Tapping Your Way to a Great Big Smile!

Emotional Freedom Technique (EFT) Tapping for Little Fingers

Ana Cybela

Illustrations by Widya Arumba

Printed in the United States of America

First Printing, 2020

ISBN 978-1-735-5694-1-3 Paperback

ISBN 978-1-735-5694-0-6 Hardcover

Kinetic Dandelions

For Sophie and Zoe

Even when I want to get up and run away, instead of finishing my homework, I still love myself. It is okay to feel bored sometimes.

Gently tap on the side of my hand. Breathe in, breathe out. I find ways to have fun no matter what I am doing.

Even when my head feels dizzy, and my tummy feels funny, I still love myself. It is okay to feel nervous sometimes.

Gently tap on the top of my head. Breathe in, breathe out. I calm my mind and relax my body.

Even when my heart feels heavy in my chest, and I don't feel like playing, I still love myself. It is okay to feel sad sometimes.

Gently tap on my eyebrows.
Breathe in, breathe out. I
find joy in the little things.

Gently tap by the sides of my eyes.
Breathe in, breathe out. If I have
to choose, I choose to be kind.

Gently tap under my eyes. Breathe in, breathe out. I
am brave and courageous. I fully trust myself.

Even when my face is turning red, and I want to hide from the world, home in bed, I still love myself. It is okay to feel embarrassed sometimes.

Gently tap under my nose. Breathe in, breathe out. I am not perfect, and I am okay with that.

Even when I don't like someone else playing with my toys, I still love myself. It is okay to feel jealous sometimes.

Gently tap on my chin.
Breathe in, breathe out.
I am happy to share,
because there is enough
for everyone.

Gently tap under my collarbones.
Breathe in, breathe out. I choose to have an
amazing day, no matter what happens.

Even when I hear a little voice inside my head, telling me that I did something wrong, I still love myself. It is okay to feel guilty sometimes.

Gently tap under my arm. Breathe in, breathe out. I forgive myself for my mistakes, because they help me learn and grow.

Even when things don't make sense to me, I still love myself. It is okay to feel confused sometimes.

Gently tap in the middle of my chest. Breathe in, breathe out. I accept things I don't understand and I learn something new every day.

As I breathe in, my tummy goes out. I am enough.

As I breathe out, my tummy goes in. I am free to be me.

Tapping: How to do it

When you're tapping your body, the rules are:

1. Pick your strongest hand. Left or right. It's up to you.
2. Whichever hand you choose, make sure to use the two fingers next to the thumb.
3. Tap about five times.

But:

Tap with one finger if you want... or three fingers.

You can tap as many times as you want.

Tapping is cool because you get to choose!

Breathing in

Sit down and get comfortable.

Now, take a long, deep breath in through your nose.

Do it nice and slowly.

Let the cool, fresh air fill your tummy like a balloon.

Breathing out

Now, blow out all the air through your mouth.

Nice and slow.

Rest your hands on your tummy.

Feel how it goes down flat as the air goes out.

Tapping the side of your hand

Use two fingers on one hand to tap on the other hand.

Imagine you're a karate expert! The bit of your hand you chop with, is where to tap.

This is the soft bit on the side of your hand underneath your little finger.

As you tap, say, "Even when I want to get up and run away, instead of finishing my homework, I still love myself. It is okay to feel bored sometimes. I find ways to have fun no matter what I am doing."

Breathe in and out slowly.

Tapping the top of your head

Tap the top of your head, right there in the middle.

As you tap, say, "Even when my head feels dizzy, and my tummy feels funny, I still love myself. It is okay to feel nervous sometimes. I calm my mind and relax my body."

Breathe in and out slowly.

Tapping your eyebrows

Tap the place where your eyebrow begins, near your nose.

As you tap, say, "Even when my heart feels heavy in my chest, and I don't feel like playing, I still love myself. It is okay to feel sad sometimes. I find joy in the little things."

Breathe in and out slowly.

Tapping the sides of your eyes

Using two fingers, touch the middle of your ear. Now slide your fingers along to the outside corner of your eye. Do you feel the bone? That's where to tap.

As you tap, say, "Even when my heart bounces like a fireball inside my chest, and my jaw clenches like a great white shark, I still love myself. It is okay to feel angry sometimes. If I have to choose, I choose to be kind."

Breathe in and out slowly.

Tapping under your eyes

With your fingers, feel the bone just below your eye. That is where to tap.

As you tap, say, "Even when my hair stands on end, and my body trembles, I still love myself. It is okay to feel scared sometimes. I am brave and courageous. I fully trust myself."

Breathe in and out slowly.

Tapping under your nose

For this one, tap in the space below your nose, but above your mouth.

There are two funny lines running down from your nose to your upper lip.

Tap right in the middle of them.

As you tap, say, "Even when my face is turning red, and I want to hide from the world, home in bed, I still love myself. It is okay to feel embarrassed sometimes. I am not perfect, and I am okay with that."

Breathe in and out slowly.

Tapping your chin

Find the spot halfway between your lower lip and the bottom of your chin.

As you tap, say, "Even when I don't like someone else playing with my toys, I still love myself. It is okay to feel jealous sometimes. I am happy to share, because there is enough for everyone."

Breathe in and out slowly.

Tapping your collarbones

This is the trickiest spot to find...
but you can do it!

Put your fingers on your shoulder.

Now slowly move them across
toward your neck.

Can you feel the thin bone near the
top of your chest?

That's your collarbone. And just
beneath it is where you need to tap.

As you tap, say, "Even when I keep
thinking about the bad things that
could happen, I still love myself. It
is okay to feel worried sometimes. I
choose to have an amazing day, no
matter what happens."

Breathe in and out slowly.

Tapping under your arm

Place your fingers in the middle of
your chest, then slide them out to
one side of your body. Now lift up
your arm. There by your armpit is
where you need to tap.

As you tap, say, "Even when I hear
a little voice inside my head, telling
me that I did something wrong, I
still love myself. It is okay to feel
guilty sometimes. I forgive myself
for my mistakes, because they help
me learn and grow."

Breathe in and out slowly.

Tapping the middle of your chest

Your heart is a little bit on the left-
hand side. Don't tap there, though.
Put your fingers on your nose and
slide them down to your chest.
There in the middle is a place called
the heart center. That is where you
need to tap.

As you tap, say, "Even when things
don't make sense to me, I still love
myself. It is okay to feel confused
sometimes. I accept things I don't
understand, and I learn something
new every day."

WORDS FOR PARENTS AND CAREGIVERS

Hello, and thank you for purchasing this book. It was written and illustrated with love, as an introduction to the world of tapping for little children. I believe that tapping has lots of benefits for overall health. We all need balance in our lives, and it's never too early to start. So, let's get those little fingers tapping and begin building the habits of a lifetime.

So, what is tapping?

Tapping, also known as Emotional Freedom Technique, or EFT for short, is a therapeutic practice that combines the ancient Chinese healing method of Acupressure, with techniques of modern psychology.

Those who practice tapping believe that our bodies operate like a transport system, with a network of interconnecting highways called meridians. Our invisible energy source flows along these highways, and when it's moving freely, we enjoy a sense of well-being in mind and body.

However, sometimes, these highways get clogged up by fear and stress. Things like anxiety, depression, insomnia, illness, a problem at work or school, or actual physical pain create negative feelings. That negativity can block or imbalance our energy flow.

So, what is tapping for?

Think of tapping as a self-healing technique that enables you to unclog your meridians, allowing the energy to flow freely through your body. In simple terms, tapping makes you feel better!

So, how does tapping work?

Tapping uses meridian points to access your energy source and restore its flow to a natural balance. By tapping on these energy hotspots, you send a message to the stress center of your brain. When you're under pressure or have negative feelings, your mind and body naturally go into survival mode. That causes stress, which can make you mentally or physically unwell.

To deal with negative thoughts, tapping is used along with affirmations, which are positive phrases that are spoken out loud. This mental and physical exercise helps kids get in touch with their feelings and encourages a positive response to their problems. The result is, they feel better about themselves through cultivating a stronger sense of self-acceptance.

Do kids need tapping?

Children and adults may have different stress triggers, but kids undoubtedly experience fear and negative feelings. Children are prone to volatile emotions, because their minds and bodies are a work in progress. Being moody and irrational can be a natural part of growing up, but kids may also feel stressed by external forces, like bullying, peer pressure, grief, or issues at home. Tapping is a coping mechanism that can help them alleviate, or even resolve, some of these problems. Some studies have found that kids may be more responsive to EFT than adults, because their issues are usually less complex and they don't question why or how tapping works. They just accept that it does!

So what's in the book?

In this book, we will identify some common negative emotions that kids may encounter in their daily lives. It is important for parents and caregivers to acknowledge and accept these emotions. This will help children feel more secure and improve their self-confidence, while becoming more receptive to the idea of tapping. For kids who cannot yet verbalize their feelings, parents and caregivers can use first-person narration to help them put their feelings into words. We will also practice a balloon-breathing exercise to help children learn to calm down and relax. In addition, we will introduce some simple and effective affirmations that can be used during tapping, to help children build self-esteem and resilience at an early age.

Tapping is a means to promote the physical and emotional well-being of your child. It might just help you as well. In fact, it will benefit your child even more, if you are able to restore your emotional balance first. It can be a fun daily exercise to do together. However, be sure not to pressure your child into practicing tapping. Simply demonstrate the techniques and let them follow your lead when they are ready. Some kids respond well to tapping with stuffed animals that have tapping points on them. Last, but not least, the illustrations in this book encourage you and your child to go outside and tap in nature, if your living environment permits. Nature amplifies the positive effects of tapping on your mental and physical health.

Tapping is not a magic bullet, but it does use your body's natural "magic buttons" to unlock the health and happiness from within.

Made in the USA
Middletown, DE
02 November 2024

63760029R00020